I AM
COURAGEOUS

Empowering Quotes for Courageous and Optimistic Living

Dr. Katherine Y. Brown

www.TrueVinePublishing.org

I Am Courageous
Dr. Katherine Y. Brown

Published by True Vine Publishing Co.
810 Dominican Dr.
Nashville, TN 37228
www.TrueVinePublishing.org

ISBN: 978-1-962783-91-0 Paperback
ISBN: 978-1-962783-15-6 eBook

Printed in the United States of America—First printing

DEDICATION

To my children, mentors, students, and YOU. Always have the courage to be seen, heard, and appreciated. Be inspired to live a courageous and optimistic life.

TABLE OF CONTENTS

INTRODUCTION

Words have an incredible impact on our lives, shaping our beliefs, thoughts, and actions. If you constantly focus on negative words and thoughts, it is likely that a negative action will follow. If you focus on positive words and thoughts, positive actions and outcomes will follow. What you say, think, believe, and do becomes your truth. By focusing on "I am" statements and affirming a belief in yourself, your goals, and your dreams you increase the possibility that you will achieve.

Affirmations centered around "I am" statements empower you to recognize your strength, embrace your potential, and cultivate belief in yourself.

Even in moments when things don't occur as planned or don't happen as fast as you want, stay focused on positive affirmations. This forms a habit of positivity that can attract great things. Live in a season of expectation, gratitude, and optimism. How you respond to situations in life is always important.

Two of the most powerful words that you can incorporate into your vocabulary to align with your purpose are, "I AM". It is my hope that you will live your life filled with purpose. You have the power within you to create the life you want.

In this book you will be introduced to a three-step framework of Recite, Reflect, and Respond to provide you with an opportunity to internalize quotes and take meaningful action towards your goals.

- **Recite**—Your **WORDS** have power.
- **Reflect**—Your **THOUGHTS** have power.
- **Respond**—Your **ACTIONS** have power.

You must be intentional and carefully consider your words, thoughts, and actions and the habits that become part of your daily routine. Every day presents you with a new opportunity for growth and self-improvement. Are you embracing each moment and the potential it holds? Do you know that the world is awaiting the unique contributions that only you can bring? There are times when you must awaken a fearless dreamer within you. This requires having optimism and courage to step into the life you envision.

Your life matters and you are on the right path towards courageous living and optimistic exploration. Thank you for taking this journey.

With gratitude and excitement,
Katherine Y. Brown, EdD, MSEd, BSOT, OTR/L

CHAPTER 1:
MASTERING THE ART OF MANIFESTATION

Three words from the book called "I Am Coura-geous" became DeVaughn's mantra. After struggling with a trembling voice, shaky hands, and experiencing bullying due to his timid style, he found comfort and strength in taking the words he read "I Am Courageous" and putting them into action. Each day, he started by af-firming, "I am courageous" in front of a mirror, he set goals to practice his public speaking, and with consis-tency for over six months, fear transformed into courage and his skills had increased.

By aligning his words (he recited), thoughts (he re-flected), and actions (he responded) with practice, even when afraid, he realized that it's more than what we say, it's what we do. I encourage you to read this book and find the courage to face any obstacle. Keep saying "I am courageous" until you believe it, transform your words, thoughts, and actions. Be resilient and manifest your dreams because just like DeVaughn, you are courageous.

↔

I recall a time when I believed that reading an affir-mation or a quote was enough to manifest my dreams. This could not be further from the truth of what I learned. My journey taught me that true growth demands more than just reading—it calls for consistent action, embrac-ing change, and a willingness to evolve. In essence, affir-

9

mations will not manifest with application. You must be courageous. This insight struck me during a period in my family life, balancing professional ambitions with raising four children. A moment of vulnerability at the kitchen table, sparked by my child's concerned question, Are you okay, Mom? which led to a transformation in my approach to life.

Well, at that moment, I was not okay. There were things that I wanted to accomplish to make life better for my children, and I was not sure what steps were needed. However, I had a choice: to continue to say what I did not have, or I could change my mindset and use my words as if I was expecting these things I wanted to come true. I needed to use positive affirmations and have the courage to live each day with intention. This epiphany drove me to start aligning my words with positive affirmations, my thoughts with clear goals, and my actions towards achieving these goals. This became more than personal change; it influenced my entire family. I started to begin each day with affirmations, instilling this practice in my children. Years later, they continue this practice in their own lives, understanding the power of words, thoughts, and actions through repetition. There is something powerful that happens when you say, "I AM."

As I progressed in my career as a speaker, coach, trainer, and mentor, these same strategies proved invaluable in helping others. Sharing my story of transforming my life with daily affirmations, I am statements, and the foundational principle of having courage, I saw a universal impact. The "Recite (words), Reflect (thoughts), and Respond (actions)" framework that I developed facilitated meaningful transformations, guiding people toward career growth and teams towards setting and achieving their collective goals.

Even in my mentoring, applying these same principles brought powerful results. Witnessing my mentees embrace these practices and achieve success reinforced my belief in these methods and fueled my goal to share them more broadly.

- Have courage.
- Be optimistic.
- Empower yourself.

This is more than a collection of affirmations. Each affirmation and reflection is intended for active engagement and ongoing growth. You are in control.

Read and try each activity with an open heart and mind. Remember, the path of life is not a one-time event but an ongoing process of self-discovery and personal development. If you invest the work and time you will see the benefits. Whether you seek personal transformation, professional growth, or to inspire others, approach this journey with courage. You have the power to make a change. You can do it.

↔

The ability to turn your aspirations into tangible outcomes is a skill. It requires a belief in your capacity to shape a reality that aligns with your goals. Using the ten themes in this book, you can explore and master the art of manifestation.

- To manifest is to bring your goals to life by transforming your dreams into reality.
- It's about aligning your thoughts, words, and actions to resonate with the outcomes you seek. You have the opportunity to see what you speak.
- It may not be easy, it may not happen as fast as you want, but you can do it.

↔

The lessons of inner strength, fearless pursuit, positivity, resilience, personal growth, abundance, authenticity, and the power of self-expression are aspects of manifestation.

- Manifestation isn't just about wishing or hoping; it's an active process and it takes hard work.
- It involves setting clear intentions, visualizing your goals, speaking powerful affirmations, and taking action.
- The steps listed below are intended to help you begin to consider how you can apply new insights. These steps are designed to guide you in creating the life you want.
-

Embrace Inner Strength
- Manifestation Step: Leverage your self-belief and inner strength to set ambitious and meaningful goals.
- Action Plan: Clearly define these goals in a journal, emphasizing their importance to you.

Pursue Dreams Fearlessly
- Manifestation Step: Take bold, decisive action towards your dreams, overcoming fear and hesitation.
- Action Plan: Identify inspired actions that align with your dreams and commit to them.

Spread Positivity
- Manifestation Step: Cultivate a positive mindset to attract positive outcomes and inspire others.
- Action Plan: Practice gratitude daily by writing down things you are thankful for.

Harness Inner Power and Resilience
- Manifestation Step: Use your resilience to navigate through challenges and stay focused on your goals.
- Action Plan: Visualize overcoming challenges and the success they lead to.

Build Self-Confidence and Grow

- Manifestation Step: Strengthen self-confidence through personal development and continuous learning.
- Action Plan: Create affirmations that affirm your capability and growth.

Overcome Challenges

- Manifestation Step: View obstacles as opportunities for growth and learning, using them to propel you forward.
- Action Plan: Regularly review your progress and adjust your approach as needed.

Embrace Transformation and Growth

- Manifestation Step: Be open to change and have the courage to modify your goals as you grow and learn more about yourself.
- Action Plan: Embrace flexibility and patience in your growth journey.

Cultivate Abundance and Prosperity

- Manifestation Step: Visualize and work towards a life of abundance, recognizing and appreciating the prosperity around you.
- Action Plan: Create a vision board to represent your abundant future.

Express Yourself Authentically

- Manifestation Step: Align your goals with your true self, ensuring that your path reflects the things that are important to you.
- Action Plan: Regularly assess if your actions and goals are in alignment with your authentic self.

Utilize Resilience and Inner Power

- Manifestation Step: Draw upon your inner strength and resilience to maintain momentum and overcome setbacks.
- Action Plan: Celebrate each small victory and step toward progress on your journey.

Remember, manifestation is not a passive process, rather it is a dynamic process of your inner world with external reality.

Now that you have begun this process, be open to the possibilities that unfold. Life often works in mysterious ways, and what manifests might sometimes be even more remarkable than what you initially envisioned. Live your life to the fullest and pursue your dreams.

CHAPTER 2

POSITIVE AFFIRMATIONS

Daily habits, particularly those involving self-talk, lay the groundwork for life's narrative. What we consistently do forms patterns, and these patterns evolve into habits. There is transformative power in positive affirmations. Consistency is key. By encouraging you to use a three-step process: recite, reflect, and respond, the goal is for you to verbalize the affirmation and also take action in a way that finds meaning for you.

To affirm is to assert something confidently, to give life to your thoughts and intentions. You are in control; practice by selecting an affirmation that resonates with you and making it a part of your daily routine. This process is not linear; you don't need to follow the steps in order. Instead, plan to dedicate time each day to one aspect of the process.

- **Recite:** Begin by verbalizing the affirmation. Let the words resonate with you, feeling their power and significance.
- **Reflect:** Next, take time to think about the meaning behind the words. How do they relate to your life, your aspirations, and your challenges?
- **Respond:** Finally, the most important step is to take action. Set a measurable goal related to your affirmation. This step allows you to transform the words into

tangible outcomes, making the affirmation a lived experience.

By committing to this practice, one step at a time, you'll see growth and change. It's about more than just saying words; it's about embedding these words and affirmations into your consciousness and letting them guide your actions.

- If you believe you can't, you can't.
- If you believe you can, you can.

Remember, growth is a journey, not a destination. Allow these affirmations to be the milestones along your path to self-discovery and empowerment. You can do it. Take it one step at a time, one day at a time, and be patient with where you are in the process. Rather than comparing yourself to others, consider that today is a new day, and you have an opportunity to live a moment in time filled with courage and optimism.

Recite: I am capable of achieving extraordinary things.

Reflect: Embrace the belief in your capacity for greatness and the extraordinary possibilities that are within you.

Respond: Today, recite this affirmation aloud three times, internalizing the belief in your ability to achieve extraordinary things. Then, identify one specific bold action you can take to move closer to your goals and commit to taking that action.

_____

_____

_____

_____

_____

_____

_____

_____

_____

_____

_____

_____

_____

Recite: I am the architect of my reality, shaping it with my beliefs.

Reflect: Recognize the power of your thoughts and beliefs in shaping your experiences and outcomes.

Respond: Today, recite this affirmation three times, reinforcing your role as the architect of your reality. Reflect on any limiting beliefs you hold and challenge them with empowering thoughts. Take one specific step towards aligning your beliefs with the reality you want to have.

_____

_____

_____

_____

_____

_____

_____

_____

_____

_____

_____

_____

_____

Recite: I am deserving of all the love, success, and abundance that life has to offer.

Reflect: Embrace your inherent worthiness of love, success, and abundance in all aspects of life.

Respond: Today, recite this affirmation three times and reaffirm that you deserve all the positive experiences life has to offer. Set a specific and intentional goal to practice acts of self-love and gratitude, and open yourself up to receive the abundance that comes your way.

_____

_____

_____

_____

_____

_____

_____

_____

_____

_____

_____

_____

Recite: I am a star, my inner light is meant to shine and inspire others.

Reflect: Acknowledge the impact of your presence and your potential to inspire and guide others.

Respond: Today, recite this affirmation aloud three times. Accept that you are special and no one was created to shine in the way that you shine. Reflect on how you can positively influence those around you and respond by taking intentional actions to uplift and inspire others.

_____

_____

_____

_____

_____

_____

_____

_____

_____

_____

_____

_____

_____

_____

21

Recite: I am resilient; every challenge I face and overcome makes me stronger.

Reflect: Embrace challenges as opportunities for growth and recognize the strength gained through resilience.

Respond: Today, recite this affirmation with determination three times, internalizing the belief in your resilience. Reflect on a recent challenge you faced and how it has contributed to your strength. Respond by actively seeking out a new challenge and approaching it with a resilient mindset.

_____

_____

_____

_____

_____

_____

_____

_____

_____

_____

_____

_____

Recite: I am fearless and will not quit in the pursuit of my dreams and aspirations.

Reflect: Release fear's grip and cultivate determination to pursue your dreams.

Respond: Today, recite this affirmation three times, removing any fear that may hold you back. Reflect on your dreams and aspirations, reaffirming your commitment to them. Respond by taking at least two fearless actions that propel you closer to realizing your dreams.

_____

_____

_____

_____

_____

_____

_____

_____

_____

_____

_____

_____

_____

_____

_____

Recite: I am a magnet for positivity, positive people, and limitless possibilities.

Reflect: Embrace the power of positivity to attract positive experiences and like-minded individuals.

Respond: Today, recite this affirmation with positivity three times, allowing your thoughts to focus on positivity. Reflect on how your energy and attitude impact the opportunities that come your way. Respond by consciously seeking out positive experiences and surrounding yourself with uplifting individuals.

_____

_____

_____

_____

_____

_____

_____

_____

_____

_____

_____

_____

Recite: I am confident in my skills, abilities, and trust the process of my growth.

Reflect: Embrace self-confidence and trust in your abilities. Recognize that growth is a continuous process and that you possess the skills and talents needed to achieve your goals.

Respond: Today, recite this affirmation with conviction three times, reinforcing your belief in your skills and abilities. Write a list of the skills and abilities that make you special.

_____

_____

_____

_____

_____

_____

_____

_____

_____

_____

_____

_____

_____

Recite: I am courageous; I embrace challenges as learning lessons or stepping stones to my greatness.

Reflect: View challenges as valuable learning opportunities and stepping stones towards reaching your highest potential.

Respond: Today, recite this affirmation with courage three times, internalizing the belief that challenges are catalysts for growth. Reflect on a recent challenge and the lessons you've gained from it. Respond by taking proactive steps towards your goals, seeing challenges as stepping stones to your greatness.

_____

_____

_____

_____

_____

_____

_____

_____

_____

_____

_____

Recite: I am unstoppable, focused, pressing forward until I achieve my goals.

Reflect: Cultivate a determination and focus that propels you towards your goals.

Respond: Today, recite this affirmation three times, igniting your inner drive. Reflect on your goals and envision yourself achieving them. Respond by setting specific goals and taking focused action towards their realization.

_____

_____

_____

_____

_____

_____

_____

_____

_____

_____

_____

_____

_____

_____

Recite: I am a person of inspiration, gratitude, and continually uplifting others with my presence.

Reflect: Recognize your ability to inspire and uplift others through acts of kindness and gratitude.

Respond: Today, recite this affirmation three times, remembering your role as a source of inspiration. Reflect on the impact you can make in the lives of others. Respond by actively seeking opportunities to uplift someone through kind words, acts of service, or offering support.

_____

_____

_____

_____

_____

_____

_____

_____

_____

_____

_____

_____

Recite: I am a positive force of nature, harnessing my internal power to create change.

Reflect: Embrace the power within you to initiate positive change in yourself and the world around you.

Respond: Today, recite this affirmation with a sense of purpose three times, igniting your passion for change. Reflect on the issues or causes that resonate with you. Respond by taking action towards creating positive change, whether through advocacy, volunteering, or implementing sustainable practices.

_____

_____

_____

_____

_____

_____

_____

_____

_____

_____

_____

_____

_____

Recite: I am bold; I take risks and step outside my comfort zone.

Reflect: Embrace the courage to take risks and venture beyond the boundaries of your comfort zone.

Respond: Today, recite this affirmation three times, reminding yourself to have courage to step into the unknown. Reflect on the areas of your life where you have been playing it safe. Respond by taking two courageous actions that push you outside of your comfort zone and open doors to growth and new opportunities.

_____

_____

_____

_____

_____

_____

_____

_____

_____

_____

_____

_____

Recite: I am resilient in the face of adversity, bouncing back with newfound strength.

Reflect: Recognize your inner resilience and the ability to rise stronger in the face of adversity.

Respond: Today, recite this affirmation three times, affirming your resilience. Reflect on a current challenge or obstacle you are facing. Respond by confronting it head-on, knowing that you have the resilience and determination to overcome it.

_____

_____

_____

_____

_____

_____

_____

_____

_____

_____

_____

_____

_____

_____

Recite: I am worthy of all the success and happiness that comes my way.

Reflect: Affirm your worthiness of success, happiness, and all the positive experiences life offers.

Respond: Today, recite this affirmation three times, reminding yourself of your inherent worthiness. Reflect on the achievements and joys in your life, recognizing that you deserve them. Respond by celebrating your worthiness and embracing every success and happiness that comes your way.

_____

_____

_____

_____

_____

_____

_____

_____

_____

_____

_____

_____

Recite: I face life's battles with determination.

Reflect: Embrace the warrior within you, equipped with determination and courage.

Respond: Today, recite this affirmation with the conviction three times, embodying your inner strength. Reflect on a difficult situation or challenge you are currently facing. Respond by confronting it with determination, knowing that you have the resilience to overcome it.

_____

_____

_____

_____

_____

_____

_____

_____

_____

_____

_____

_____

_____

_____

Recite: I am limitless; there are no boundaries to what I can achieve.

Reflect: Recognize the potential within you and release self-imposed limitations.

Respond: Today, recite this affirmation with boundless belief three times, expanding your perception of what is possible. Reflect on any self-imposed limitations that may be holding you back. Respond by taking inspired action towards a goal or dream that stretches the boundaries of your imagination.

_____

_____

_____

_____

_____

_____

_____

_____

_____

_____

_____

_____

Recite: I am a creator, manifesting my dreams into reality.

Reflect: Embrace your creative power to turn your dreams and visions into tangible manifestations.

Respond: Today, recite this affirmation with creative intent three times, unleashing your creative potential. Reflect on a dream or vision you have and visualize it as a tangible reality. Respond by taking specific steps or creating a plan that moves you closer to manifesting your dreams.

_____

_____

_____

_____

_____

_____

_____

_____

_____

_____

_____

_____

Recite: I am a source of inspiration, empowering others to embrace their greatness.

Reflect: Acknowledge your ability to inspire and empower others to recognize and embrace their own greatness.

Respond: Today, recite this affirmation with genuine enthusiasm three times, radiating your inner light. Reflect on the impact you can make in the lives of others. Respond by seeking opportunities to inspire and uplift others, sharing your wisdom, and offering support and encouragement.

_____

_____

_____

_____

_____

_____

_____

_____

_____

_____

_____

Recite: I am an agent of change, making a positive impact on the world around me.

Reflect: Embrace your role as an agent of change and the power you possess to make a positive difference.

Respond: Today, recite this affirmation with a sense of purpose three times, igniting your passion for transformation. Reflect on the changes you wish to see in the world. Respond by taking action towards creating positive change, whether through volunteering, raising awareness, or engaging in acts of kindness.

_____

_____

_____

_____

_____

_____

_____

_____

_____

_____

_____

_____

Recite: I am confident in my unique gifts and share them with the world.

Reflect: Embrace and celebrate your unique gifts and talents, recognizing their value and importance.

Respond: Today, recite this affirmation with confidence three times, owning your unique gifts. Reflect on the ways you can share your gifts with the world. Respond by taking a bold step to share your talents, whether through creative expression, teaching, mentoring, or offering your skills to others.

_____

_____

_____

_____

_____

_____

_____

_____

_____

_____

_____

_____

Recite: I am a catalyst for transformation, embracing growth with open arms.

Reflect: Embrace your role as a catalyst for personal and collective transformation, and welcome growth as a necessary part of your journey.

Respond: Today, recite this affirmation with enthusiasm three times, focusing on your passion for growth and transformation. Reflect on areas of your life where you want growth and positive change. Respond by taking intentional action towards your personal development, embracing new experiences, or seeking opportunities for learning and growth.

_____

_____

_____

_____

_____

_____

_____

_____

_____

_____

Recite: I am the architect of my destiny, creating a life of abundance and fulfillment.

Reflect: Recognize that you have the power to determine your goals.

Respond: Today, recite this affirmation three times, empowering yourself as the architect of your destiny. Reflect on your vision for an abundant and fulfilling life. Respond by setting clear intentions and taking inspired action aligned with your goals.

_____

_____

_____

_____

_____

_____

_____

_____

_____

_____

_____

_____

_____

Recite: I am an image of health and vitality, radiating wellness from the inside out.

Reflect: Visualize yourself as a healthy individual embodying well-being in every aspect of your being.

Respond: Today, recite this affirmation three times, embodying the image of health and vitality. Reflect on the actions you can take to enhance your well-being. Respond by engaging in activities that nourish your body, mind, and spirit.

_____

_____

_____

_____

_____

_____

_____

_____

_____

_____

_____

_____

_____

Recite: I am prosperous in all areas of my life, embracing abundance and gratitude.

Reflect: Embrace a mindset of abundance and gratitude, recognizing the prosperity that exists in all aspects of life.

Respond: Today, recite this affirmation gratitude three times, cultivating a deep sense of abundance. Reflect on the abundance that already exists in your life. Respond by expressing gratitude for the blessings you have and finding ways to share your abundance with others.

_____

_____

_____

_____

_____

_____

_____

_____

_____

_____

_____

Recite: I am resilient; setbacks are merely stepping stones on my path to success.

Reflect: View setbacks as valuable stepping stones on your journey towards success and personal growth.

Respond: Today, recite this affirmation with resilience three times, embracing setbacks as opportunities for growth. Reflect on a recent setback and the lessons you learned from it. Respond by taking proactive steps to overcome the setback and continue moving forward on your path to success.

_____

_____

_____

_____

_____

_____

_____

_____

_____

_____

_____

_____

_____

Recite: I am the guardian of my well-being, prioritizing self-care and cultivating a healthy lifestyle.

Reflect: Recognize your responsibility in prioritizing your well-being and taking care of yourself on all levels.

Respond: Today, recite this affirmation with self-care in mind three times, affirming your commitment to your well-being. Reflect on the self-care practices that nourish you physically, mentally, and emotionally. Respond by engaging in at least two self-care activities that promote your overall well-being.

Recite: I am prosperous; my financial abundance grows with each positive intention and action.

Reflect: Cultivate a mindset of financial abundance, knowing that your positive intentions and actions contribute to your prosperity.

Respond: Today, recite this affirmation with confidence three times, aligning yourself with the energy of financial abundance. Reflect on the positive financial intentions you have and the actions you can take to support your prosperity. Respond by taking at least one action that moves you closer to your financial goals.

_____

_____

_____

_____

_____

_____

_____

_____

_____

_____

_____

Recite: I am resilient; I rise above challenges and tap into my inner power to overcome.

Reflect: Embrace your resilience and tap into your inner power to overcome challenges.

Respond: Today, recite this affirmation with determination three times, igniting your inner strength. Reflect on a recent challenge or obstacle you faced and how you overcame it. Respond by taking proactive steps to tackle a current challenge, drawing upon your resilience and inner power.

Recite: I am abundant in all aspects of my life, embracing prosperity with an open heart.

Reflect: Embrace the belief in abundance and open yourself up to receive prosperity in all areas of your life.

Respond: Today, recite this affirmation with an open heart three times, allowing the energy of abundance to flow through you. Reflect on the areas of your life where you want abundance and prosperity. Respond by taking positive actions that align with the abundance you wish to attract.

_____

_____

_____

_____

_____

_____

_____

_____

_____

_____

_____

_____

_____

Recite: I am resilient; I adapt, evolve, and thrive in the ever-changing landscape of life.

Reflect: Embrace your ability to adapt, evolve, and thrive amidst the changes and challenges of life.

Respond: Today, recite this affirmation with adaptability three times, embodying your resilience. Reflect on a recent change or transition you experienced and how you adapted to it. Respond by embracing change and actively seeking opportunities for growth and expansion.

_____

_____

_____

_____

_____

_____

_____

_____

_____

_____

_____

_____

_____

Recite: I am centered and grounded, finding peace and clarity within myself.

Reflect: Cultivate a sense of inner peace and clarity, grounding yourself amidst life's demands.

Respond: Today, recite this affirmation with serenity three times, connecting with your inner center. Reflect on the practices or rituals that help you feel grounded and find peace within yourself. Respond by engaging in at least one grounding practice or mindfulness exercise to foster inner peace and clarity.

_____

_____

_____

_____

_____

_____

_____

_____

_____

_____

_____

_____

_____

Recite: I am a catalyst for positive change, inspiring others to step into their power.

Reflect: Recognize your role as a catalyst for positive change and the power of your influence on others.

Respond: Today, recite this affirmation with purpose three times, embracing your ability to inspire others. Reflect on the positive change you wish to see in the world and how you can contribute to it. Respond by actively engaging in conversations, actions, or initiatives that empower and uplift others.

_____

_____

_____

_____

_____

_____

_____

_____

_____

_____

_____

_____

_____

Recite: I am confident in my unique voice, sharing it authentically with the world.

Reflect: Embrace and celebrate your unique voice, knowing that it has the power to make a positive impact.

Respond: Today, recite this affirmation with authenticity three times, embodying the confidence in expressing your true self. Reflect on the unique gifts, talents, and perspectives you bring to the world. Respond by sharing your voice in a meaningful way, whether through writing, speaking, creating, or engaging in conversations that matter to you.

_____

_____

_____

_____

_____

_____

_____

_____

_____

_____

Recite: I am a co-creator with the universe, manifesting my goals with intention.

Reflect: Recognize your role as a co-creator with the universe, manifesting your goals.

Respond: Today, recite this affirmation with focused intention three times, aligning yourself with the creative forces of the universe. Reflect on your goals. Respond by setting clear intentions and taking inspired actions that align with your vision, trusting in the co-creative process with the universe.

_____

_____

_____

_____

_____

_____

_____

_____

_____

_____

BELIEVE IN YOURSELF.
RECITE THIS THREE
TIMES—
"I AM COURAGEOUS"

CHAPTER 3:
EMBRACING YOUR INNER STRENGTH

Consider the journey you've been on, the challenges you've faced, and the moments when your inner strength shined through. When did you feel this strength most? Was it during a time of trial (the hardest) or a moment of triumph (the success)? These experiences, both big and small, are testimonies to the resilience you possess. Take some time to reflect deeply on these moments.

Think about the lessons learned and how they've shaped your understanding of your own strength. Journaling about these experiences will not only affirm your resilience but also inspire you to draw upon this inner strength in future endeavors. Every experience has an opportunity for growth, what did you learn? You have the power to achieve extraordinary things. Reflect on your inner strength and how it guides you through life's journey.

HAVE THE COURAGE TO JOURNAL

I AM CAPABLE OF ACHIEVING EXTRAORDINARY THINGS.

Reflection: Envision a challenging goal. How can your inner strength assist in achieving it?

_____

_____

_____

_____

_____

_____

_____

_____

I AM THE ARCHITECT OF MY REALITY, SHAPING IT WITH MY BELIEFS.

Reflection: How have your beliefs shaped your life? What belief change can lead to a positive outcome?

_____

_____

_____

_____

_____

_____

_____

_____

_____

_____

_____

I AM DESERVING ABUNDANCE, LOVE, AND SUCCESS.

Reflection: What does love, success, and abundance mean to you? How can you be more receptive to these?

_____

_____

_____

_____

_____

_____

_____

_____

_____

_____

_____

I CREATE A PATH AND NEW OPPORTUNITIES FOR OTHERS TO FOLLOW.

Reflection: In what ways can you serve as a source of inspiration for others?

_____

_____

_____

_____

_____

_____

_____

_____

_____

_____

I AM RESILIENT; EVERY CHALLENGE I FACE AND OVERCOME MAKES ME STRONGER.

Reflection: Recall a recent challenge and how overcoming it has made you stronger.

_____

_____

_____

_____

_____

_____

_____

_____

_____

CHAPTER 4:
FEARLESS PURSUIT OF DREAMS

Every dream starts with a spark, a whisper of what if. But often, it's our own fears that cloud these sparks. Think about the dreams that excite you that you don't pursue. What would you pursue if fear were not a factor?

Reflect on the barriers, both internal and external, that may have held you back. This chapter is a space for you to confront these fears, to lay them out on paper, and to strategize ways to overcome them. Your dreams are more than just thoughts; they are the blueprints of your future. Embrace them with courage, and use this space to map out the steps to bring them to fruition. You can have a positive impact on your own life by pursuing your dreams.

I AM FEARLESS AND WILL NOT QUIT IN THE PURSUIT OF MY DREAMS AND ASPIRATIONS.

Reflection: Identify a fear holding you back and strategize how to overcome it.

_____

_____

_____

_____

_____

_____

_____

_____

_____

_____

_____

_____

I AM A MAGNET FOR POSITIVITY, POSITIVE PEOPLE, AND LIMITLESS POSSIBILITIES.

Reflection: Reflect on the positive forces in your life. How can you cultivate more positivity?

_____

_____

_____

_____

_____

_____

_____

_____

_____

_____

_____

I AM CONFIDENT IN MY SKILLS, ABILITIES, AND TRUST THE PROCESS OF MY GROWTH.

Reflection: Think about a skill you've honed and its role in your personal growth.

_____

_____

_____

_____

_____

_____

_____

_____

_____

_____

_____

I AM COURAGEOUS; I EMBRACE CHALLENGES AS LEARNING LESSONS OR STEPPING STONES TO MY GREATNESS.

Reflection: View a current challenge as an opportunity. How does this change your approach?

_____

_____

_____

_____

_____

_____

_____

_____

_____

I AM UNSTOPPABLE, FOCUSED, PRESSING FORWARD UNTIL I ACHIEVE MY DESIRED OUTCOMES.

Reflection: Consider an objective you're passionately pursuing. How does your focus contribute to your progress?

_____

_____

_____

_____

_____

_____

_____

_____

_____

_____

CHAPTER 5:
INSPIRING OTHERS AND SPREADING POSITIVITY

Recall a moment when someone's act of kindness or words of encouragement brightened your day. How did their positivity impact you? You possess the same ability to be a source of inspiration and positivity in the lives of others. Consider the ways your actions, words, and presence can uplift and inspire those around you.

Journal about specific instances where you've been a positive influence and how you can continue to spread this light. This reflection isn't just about recognizing your impact; it's about actively seeking ways to be a source of positivity and hope in your community and beyond. You can have a positive impact on others and the world. As you read these affirmations, consider how you can encourage and uplift those around you.

Reflection: Describe way you have recently inspired or positively influenced someone in your life. What did you learn from this that you can apply in a different area of your life?

_____

_____

_____

_____

_____

_____

_____

_____

_____

I AM A POSITIVE FORCE OF NATURE, HARNESSING MY INTERNAL POWER TO CREATE CHANGE.

Reflection: Reflect on a situation where your positive attitude made a difference.

_____

_____

_____

_____

_____

_____

_____

_____

_____

_____

_____

_____

I AM BOLD; I DARE TO TAKE RISKS AND STEP OUTSIDE MY COMFORT ZONE.

Reflection: Recall a moment when stepping out of your comfort zone led to personal growth or success.

_____

_____

_____

_____

_____

_____

_____

_____

_____

_____

_____

_____

_____

I AM RESILIENT IN THE FACE OF ADVERSITY, BOUNCING BACK WITH NEWFOUND STRENGTH.

Reflection: Consider a tough situation you faced and how you emerged stronger from it.

_____

_____

_____

_____

_____

_____

_____

_____

_____

_____

_____

_____

I AM WORTHY OF ALL THE SUCCESS AND HAPPINESS THAT COMES MY WAY.

Reflection: Identify a recent success or happy moment and acknowledge your worthiness.

_____

_____

_____

_____

_____

_____

_____

_____

_____

_____

_____

_____

CHAPTER 6:
CULTIVATING INNER POWER AND RESILIENCE

Life's challenges test our strength and resilience. Think about the times you've faced adversity head-on and emerged stronger. What did these challenges teach you about your inner power? Reflect on how these experiences shaped your character, your resilience, and prepared you for future obstacles.

Acknowledge and celebrate your journey of overcoming. Explore and deepen your understanding of your inner strength, learning to harness it in both challenging and everyday situations. Recognize the limitless potential within you. As you explore these quotes, think about how you can tap into your inner power and resilience to overcome life's challenges.

I AM A WARRIOR, FACING LIFE'S BATTLES WITH DETERMINATION.

Reflection: Think of a challenge you're currently facing and how you can confront it with determination.

_____

_____

_____

_____

_____

_____

_____

_____

_____

_____

_____

_____

_____

I AM LIMITLESS; THERE ARE NO BOUNDARIES TO WHAT I CAN ACHIEVE.

Reflection: Envision a goal that seems beyond reach and how you might achieve it with persistence.

_____

_____

_____

_____

_____

_____

_____

_____

_____

_____

_____

_____

_____

I AM A CREATOR, MANIFESTING MY DREAMS INTO REALITY.

Reflection: Reflect on a dream you have and the steps you can take to make it a reality.

_____

_____

_____

_____

_____

_____

_____

_____

_____

_____

_____

_____

_____

_____

I AM A SOURCE OF INSPIRATION, EMPOWERING OTHERS TO EMBRACE THEIR GREATNESS.

Reflection: Consider how you can use your experiences to inspire and uplift others.

_____

_____

_____

_____

_____

_____

_____

_____

_____

_____

_____

I AM AN AGENT OF CHANGE, MAKING A POSITIVE IMPACT ON THE WORLD AROUND ME.

Reflection: Identify one small action you can take to positively impact your immediate environment.

_____

_____

_____

_____

_____

_____

_____

_____

_____

_____

_____

_____

CHAPTER 7:
SELF-CONFIDENCE AND PERSONAL GROWTH

Self-confidence is often developed in moments of success and achievement. Think back to times when you felt a strong sense of accomplishment. What strengths did you draw upon? Reflect on these experiences, to uncover the roots of your confidence, and to nurture it further. Consider how these moments have contributed to your personal growth and self-understanding. Your triumphs and the strengths you exhibited can help reinforce your self-confidence and encourage you to embrace new growth opportunities with open arms. Embrace the journey of self-discovery and growth.

I AM CONFIDENT IN MY UNIQUE GIFTS AND SHARE THEM WITH THE WORLD.

Reflection: Identify a unique talent or quality you have and how you can utilize it more.

_____

_____

_____

_____

_____

_____

_____

_____

_____

_____

_____

I AM A CATALYST FOR TRANSFORMATION, EMBRACING GROWTH WITH OPEN ARMS.

Reflection: Think of a recent experience that sparked personal growth or transformation.

_____

_____

_____

_____

_____

_____

_____

_____

_____

_____

I AM RESILIENT; SETBACKS FUEL MY DETERMINATION TO SUCCEED.

Reflection: Consider a setback you've experienced and how it has strengthened your resolve.

_____

_____

_____

_____

_____

_____

_____

_____

_____

_____

_____

_____

I AM PRIORITIZING SELF-CARE AND CULTIVATING A HEALTHY LIFESTYLE.

Reflection: Write one goal to improve your mental and physical health. Then describe your plan for the next 30 days to make progress toward this goal. What will you do each day?

_____

_____

_____

_____

_____

_____

_____

_____

_____

_____

_____

I AM PROSPEROUS IN ALL AREAS OF MY LIFE, EMBRACING ABUNDANCE WITH GRATITUDE.

Reflection: Think of an aspect of your life where you feel abundant and express gratitude for it.

_____

_____

_____

_____

_____

_____

_____

_____

_____

_____

_____

_____

CHAPTER 8:
OVERCOMING CHALLENGES AND ADVERSITY

Each challenge we face is a stepping stone towards resilience and expanded wisdom. Take the time to reflect on the significant challenges that have shaped your life's narrative. How have these experiences molded you into the person you are today? Journaling about moments of adversity is not just about recounting difficulties; it's about recognizing the strength and perseverance you displayed. It's about understanding that each challenge was an opportunity for growth and transformation. Everything you journal about is a testament to your resilience, a reminder that you have the power to turn adversity into a source of strength. Life's challenges are opportunities for growth. Consider how you can overcome obstacles and transform adversity into strength.

I AM RESILIENT; SETBACKS ARE STEPPING STONES ON MY PATH TO SUCCESS.

Reflection: Reflect on a recent setback and how it can be a stepping stone to greater success.

_____

_____

_____

_____

_____

_____

_____

_____

_____

_____

_____

_____

_____

I AM THE FUTURE OF GOOD HEALTH, ATTRACTING WELLNESS AND VITALITY INTO MY LIFE.

Reflection: Consider the steps you can take today to enhance your physical and mental well-being.

_____

_____

_____

_____

_____

_____

_____

_____

_____

_____

_____

I AM COMMITTED TO MY HEALTH.

Reflection: Identify one self-care practice you can incorporate into your daily routine for better health.

_____

_____

_____

_____

_____

_____

_____

_____

_____

_____

_____

_____

_____

I AM DEBT FREE.

Reflection: Think of one positive financial habit you can start to enhance your prosperity.

_____

_____

_____

_____

_____

_____

_____

_____

_____

_____

_____

_____

_____

_____

_____

I AM THE MASTER OF MY FATE, STEERING MY LIFE TOWARDS POSITIVE AND FULFILLING OUTCOMES.

Reflection: Consider how the choices you make daily impact your life's direction. What choices can lead you towards more positive and fulfilling outcomes?

_____

_____

_____

_____

_____

_____

_____

_____

_____

_____

CHAPTER 9:
TRANSFORMATION AND GROWTH

Change is the only constant in life, and our response to it shapes our journey. Throughout our lives, we encounter moments of transformation that test our resilience. Reflect on these times in your life. How did you adapt?

What strategies did you use during these periods of uncertainty? Our responses to challenges teach us lessons about ourselves and the world around us. Reflecting on these lessons isn't a one-time activity; it's a continuous process. Embracing transformation often requires courage to face the unknown.

It's in these moments that we have the opportunity to evolve. As you take time to reflect, consider the changes you've endured and how they have contributed to the person you've become. Recognize the strengths you've gained. There is an opportunity to not just survive, but to thrive—embrace it.

I AM A CATALYST FOR POSITIVE CHANGE, CONSTANTLY EVOLVING AND GROWING.

Reflection: Think about an area in your life where you've seen significant growth. What led to this change?

_____

_____

_____

_____

_____

_____

_____

_____

_____

_____

_____

I AM ON A JOURNEY OF CONTINUOUS IMPROVEMENT, LEARNING AND EXPANDING MY HORIZONS.

Reflection: Identify a new skill or knowledge area you want to explore to foster your personal growth.

_____

_____

_____

_____

_____

_____

_____

_____

_____

_____

_____

I AM EMBRACING THE UNKNOWN, TRUSTING THAT IT LEADS TO PERSONAL TRANSFORMATION.

Reflection: Reflect on a time when stepping into the unknown led to positive transformation in your life.

_____

_____

_____

_____

_____

_____

_____

_____

_____

_____

_____

_____

I AM COMMITTED TO MY PERSONAL DEVELOPMENT, UNDERSTANDING IT'S A LIFELONG JOURNEY.

Reflection: How can you make personal development a consistent part of your daily routine?

_____

_____

_____

_____

_____

_____

_____

_____

_____

_____

_____

I AM EVOLVING WITH EVERY EXPERIENCE, GROWING WISER AND STRONGER.

Reflection: Consider a recent experience and the wisdom or strength you gained from it.

_____

_____

_____

_____

_____

_____

_____

_____

_____

_____

_____

_____

CHAPTER 10:
ABUNDANCE AND PROSPERITY

Abundance is a concept that can be enriched by the practice of gratitude. Financial abundance isn't only about the amount in your bank account; it's about appreciating and wisely managing your resources, acknowledging every asset as a blessing. Community abundance can be expressed within relationships, recognizing that every interaction adds value to our collective well-being and community growth.

Gratitude for personal achievements allows us to celebrate our growth and milestones, seeing them as collective victories rather than isolated events. And finally, gratitude for our health is an often overlooked aspect of well-being. Each of these aspects, can be approached with gratitude and prosperity.

I AM PROSPEROUS; MY FINANCIAL ABUNDANCE GROWS WITH EACH POSITIVE INTENTION AND ACTION.

Reflection: What small steps can you take today to improve your financial well-being?

_____

_____

_____

_____

_____

_____

_____

_____

_____

_____

_____

I AM RESILIENT; I RISE ABOVE CHALLENGES AND TAP INTO MY POWER TO OVERCOME.

Reflection: How can resilience contribute to your sense of abundance and prosperity?

_____

_____

_____

_____

_____

_____

_____

_____

_____

_____

_____

_____

I AM THE FUTURE OF GOOD HEALTH, ATTRACTING WELLNESS AND VITALITY INTO MY LIFE.

Reflection: What does wellness and vitality look like for you, and how can you achieve it?

_____

_____

_____

_____

_____

_____

_____

_____

_____

_____

I AM ABUNDANT IN ALL ASPECTS OF MY LIFE, EMBRACING PROSPERITY WITH AN OPEN HEART.

Reflection: Reflect on an area of your life where you feel particularly abundant. What makes it so?

_____

_____

_____

_____

_____

_____

_____

_____

_____

_____

I AM A VESSEL OF RESILIENCE, TRANSFORMING ADVERSITY INTO GROWTH.

Reflection: Think of a recent adversity. How can you transform this experience into an opportunity for growth?

_____

_____

_____

_____

_____

_____

_____

_____

_____

_____

_____

CHAPTER 11:
SELF-EXPRESSION AND AUTHENTICITY

Authentic self-expression is one of the purest forms of personal freedom. Think about moments when you felt aligned with your authentic self. What did those moments feel like? How did expressing your true self impact your life and those around you? Take time to explore and celebrate your unique identity. Embrace the journey of authenticity, finding joy and fulfillment in being unapologetically you. You are special, consider how you can more fully express your true self.

I AM CONFIDENT IN MY UNIQUE VOICE, SHARING IT AUTHENTICALLY WITH THE WORLD.

Reflection: What does expressing your authentic self look like, and how can you practice it more?

_____

_____

_____

_____

_____

_____

_____

_____

_____

_____

_____

I AM MANIFESTING MY GOALS WITH INTENTION.

Reflection: Think about a goal you wish to manifest. What intentional steps can you take towards it?

_____

_____

_____

_____

_____

_____

_____

_____

_____

_____

_____

_____

_____

Reflection: Reflect on how your resilience has shaped your personal journey.

_____

_____

_____

_____

_____

_____

_____

_____

_____

_____

_____

_____

I AM THE EMBODIMENT OF HEALTH AND VITALITY, NURTURING MY BODY, MIND, AND SPIRIT.

Reflection: How can nurturing your health and vitality aid in your self-expression?

_____

_____

_____

_____

_____

_____

_____

_____

_____

_____

I AM PROSPEROUS IN ALL ASPECTS OF MY LIFE, EMBRACING ABUNDANCE WITH GRATITUDE.

Reflection: How does embracing abundance in different areas of your life enhance your self-expression?

_____

_____

_____

_____

_____

_____

_____

_____

_____

_____

_____

CHAPTER 12:
RESILIENCE AND INNER POWER

Inner strength is a vital resource we often tap into during challenging times. Reflect on moments when you've used this power; how did harnessing it feel? Consider how your resilience has not only helped you face past challenges but also how it serves as a blueprint for future successes. As you consider your inner strength think about how you can turn it into a source of empowerment and inspiration. Have courage and believe in your ability to use the power within you to rise above challenges.

I AM RESILIENT; I RISE ABOVE CHALLENGES AND TAP INTO MY INNER POWER TO OVERCOME.

Reflection: Think about a current challenge and how your inner strength can help you overcome it.

_____

_____

_____

_____

_____

_____

_____

_____

_____

_____

_____

_____

I AM THE FUTURE OF GOOD HEALTH, ATTRACTING WELLNESS AND VITALITY INTO MY LIFE.

Reflection: What wellness practices can you adopt to strengthen your inner power?

_____

_____

_____

_____

_____

_____

_____

_____

_____

_____

_____

I AM ABUNDANT IN ALL ASPECTS OF MY LIFE, EMBRACING PROSPERITY WITH AN OPEN HEART.

Reflection: How does embracing abundance help you tap into your inner power?

_____

_____

_____

_____

_____

_____

_____

_____

_____

_____

_____

I AM RESILIENT; SETBACKS ARE MERELY STEPPING STONES ON MY PATH TO SUCCESS.

Reflection: How can viewing setbacks as stepping stones change your approach to challenges?

_____

_____

_____

_____

_____

_____

_____

_____

_____

_____

_____

I AM THE ARCHITECT OF MY DESTINY, CREATING A LIFE OF ABUNDANCE AND FULFILLMENT.

Reflection: What steps can you take to actively shape your destiny towards abundance and fulfillment?

_____

_____

_____

_____

_____

_____

_____

_____

_____

_____

CHAPTER 13:
CONTINUE THE JOURNEY

Reflecting back, as I shared earlier, I remember a time when I thought merely reading an affirmation or a quote would be enough to manifest my dreams. However, my experiences taught me that true growth is about much more than just reading—it requires consistent action, embracing change, and a willingness to evolve. The affirmations and processes in this book have been tested not only in my personal journey but also in my work with mentees, coaching sessions, educators, and professionals from diverse backgrounds. Quotes and affirmations demand your active participation to unlock their full potential.

As long as you're willing to open the pages of this book, it can serve as a dynamic tool in your life. It's designed for revisiting, with each affirmation and reflection crafted to inspire action and foster personal growth. As you face new challenges and grow through your experiences, these pages will provide evolving insights and renewed motivation. Remember, it's okay for your insights to change as you do; embrace this process and respect where you are in your journey.

As you grow, your perspective on these affirmations may also naturally shift, revealing your path of self-discovery. As you evolve, it is a clear indicator of your personal development. Let's be clear, there is no right or wrong, this is your path, your shift, and the new story that only you can write.

Embrace your inner strength and act on your dreams. Each day is a new chance to live with courage and optimism. Continue moving forward, learning, and growing. Let this book be your constant companion, a reminder of the extraordinary life you're capable of creating. Trust in the process, stay committed to consistency, and remember: your journey is a continuously unfolding adventure. You can do it!

JOURNAL

_____

_____

_____

_____

_____

_____

_____

_____

_____

_____

_____

_____

_____

_____

_____

_____

_____

_____

_____

_____

www.ingramcontent.com/pod-product-compliance
Lightning Source LLC
Chambersburg PA
CBHW051005140626
46546CB00016B/877